A vegan recipes cookbook is a compilation of delicious and nutritious plant-based meals that do not include any animal products or byproducts such as meat, dairy, eggs, honey, or gelatin. It is designed to provide a variety of options for those who follow a vegan diet, whether for ethical, health, or environmental reasons.

A vegan recipes cookbook typically features a diverse range of dishes that showcase the versatility of plant-based ingredients. It includes appetizers, main courses, side dishes, salads, soups, stews, desserts, and more, with a focus on using fresh, whole-food ingredients to create flavorful and satisfying meals.

The cookbook may also provide tips on meal planning, ingredient substitutions, and techniques for cooking and baking without animal products. It may include recipes that are quick and easy to make, as well as more elaborate dishes for special occasions.

Overall, a vegan recipes cookbook is a valuable resource for anyone looking to incorporate more plant-based meals into their diet and explore the delicious and nutritious world of vegan cuisine.

# Buddha Bowl

Ingredients:

1 large sweet potato, peeled and chopped into bite-sized pieces
1 can chickpeas, drained and rinsed
1 cup uncooked brown rice
4 cups water
4-6 cups kale, destemmed and chopped
4-6 radishes, sliced
2-3 carrots, peeled and sliced
1/4 head of cabbage, chopped
2-3 tbsp olive oil
Salt and pepper, to taste

Instructions:

Preheat your oven to 400°F (200°C).
In a medium pot, add the uncooked brown rice and 4 cups of water. Bring to a boil, reduce heat to low, and simmer for 40-45 minutes, or until the rice is tender and cooked through.
While the rice is cooking, prepare the sweet potatoes and chickpeas. Place them in a large mixing bowl and toss with 1-2 tbsp olive oil, salt, and pepper to taste.
Spread the sweet potatoes and chickpeas in a single layer on a baking sheet lined with parchment paper. Roast for 20-25 minutes, or until the sweet potatoes are tender and the chickpeas are crispy.
While the sweet potatoes and chickpeas are roasting, prepare the kale, radishes, carrots, and cabbage. Add them to a large mixing bowl and massage them with 1-2 tbsp olive oil, salt, and pepper to taste.
Divide the cooked brown rice among 4 bowls. Top with the roasted sweet potatoes and chickpeas, and the massaged kale, radishes, carrots, and cabbage.
Serve and enjoy! Optional: garnish with additional chopped walnuts and your favorite dressing.

# Delicious Rice Bliss Bowl

Here's how you can prepare a delicious rice bliss bowl:

## Ingredients:

1 cup brown rice
2 cups water
1 block of tempeh, sliced
1 tablespoon soy sauce
1 tablespoon sesame oil
1/2 teaspoon garlic powder
1/2 teaspoon onion powder
1/2 teaspoon smoked paprika
1/2 cup kimchi
1/2 cup shredded carrots
1/2 cup shredded red cabbage
1/4 cup roasted peanuts, chopped
Fresh cilantro for garnish

## For the peanut sauce:

1/4 cup natural peanut butter
2 tablespoons soy sauce
1 tablespoon maple syrup
1 tablespoon rice vinegar
1/2 teaspoon sesame oil
1/2 teaspoon sriracha sauce (optional)
Water to thin as needed

## Instructions:

Rinse the brown rice and place it in a medium-sized pot with 2 cups of water. Bring it to a boil over high heat, then lower the heat and let it simmer for 35-40 minutes, or until the rice is tender and cooked through.

In the meantime, preheat a grill or grill pan over medium-high heat. In a small bowl, mix together soy sauce, sesame oil, garlic powder, onion powder, and smoked paprika. Brush the tempeh slices with the mixture and place them on the grill. Cook for 2-3 minutes per side, or until nicely charred and crispy.

To make the peanut sauce, whisk together peanut butter, soy sauce, maple syrup, rice vinegar, sesame oil, and sriracha sauce (if using) in a small bowl. Add water as needed to thin the sauce to your desired consistency.

To assemble the bowl, divide the cooked rice among four bowls. Top with grilled tempeh, kimchi, shredded carrots, shredded cabbage, and chopped peanuts. Drizzle the peanut sauce over the top of each bowl and garnish with fresh cilantro leaves. Enjoy your delicious and healthy rice bliss bowl!

# Roasted Veggie Grain Bowl

## Ingredients:

1 small sweet potato, peeled and cubed
1 small head of broccoli, chopped into florets
1 small red onion, diced
1 red bell pepper, diced
2 tablespoons olive oil
1 teaspoon salt
1 teaspoon black pepper
1 cup quinoa, rinsed and drained
2 cups vegetable broth or water
1/4 cup pepitas (pumpkin seeds)

## For the Kale Pesto:

2 cups packed kale leaves, stems removed
1/2 cup walnuts
1/4 cup nutritional yeast
3 garlic cloves
1/2 cup olive oil
1/2 teaspoon salt
1/2 teaspoon black pepper

## Instructions:

Preheat the oven to 400°F (200°C).
In a large bowl, combine the sweet potato, broccoli, red onion, red bell pepper, olive oil, salt, and black pepper. Toss to coat the vegetables evenly.
Spread the vegetables out in a single layer on a baking sheet. Roast for 20-25 minutes, or until the vegetables are tender and browned in spots.
While the vegetables are roasting, prepare the quinoa. In a medium saucepan, bring the quinoa and vegetable broth or water to a boil over high heat. Reduce the heat to low, cover the saucepan, and simmer for 15-20 minutes, or until the liquid is absorbed and the quinoa is tender.
In a small dry skillet, toast the pepitas over medium heat for 2-3 minutes, or until they are lightly browned and fragrant.
To make the kale pesto, combine the kale leaves, walnuts, nutritional yeast, garlic, olive oil, salt, and black pepper in a food processor. Pulse until the mixture is smooth and creamy.
To assemble the bowls, divide the cooked quinoa and roasted vegetables among four bowls. Drizzle each bowl with some of the kale pesto and sprinkle with toasted pepitas.
Serve immediately and enjoy!

# Cauliflower Rice

Here's how to make cauliflower rice:

Ingredients:

1 head of cauliflower
1 tablespoon olive oil
Salt and pepper to taste

- Instructions:
- 
- Wash and dry the cauliflower head.
- Cut off the florets from the stem and discard the stem.
- Place the cauliflower florets in a food processor and pulse until they resemble rice.
- Heat the olive oil in a large skillet over medium-high heat.
- Add the cauliflower rice to the skillet and stir to combine with the oil.
- Season with salt and pepper to taste.
- Cook for 5-7 minutes, stirring occasionally, until the cauliflower rice is tender and slightly golden brown.
- Remove from heat and use as a base for your grain-free grain bowl.

# Veggie Burger

Here's a recipe for a delicious veggie burger:

### Ingredients:

1 can of black beans, drained and rinsed
1/2 cup of cooked quinoa
1/2 cup of breadcrumbs
1/2 onion, diced
2 garlic cloves, minced
1 tsp of chili powder
1 tsp of cumin
Salt and pepper to taste
1 tbsp of olive oil
4 burger buns
Toppings of your choice (lettuce, tomato, avocado, etc.)

### Instructions:

In a large mixing bowl, mash the black beans with a fork or potato masher until they are mostly smooth, but still have some texture.
Add in the quinoa, breadcrumbs, onion, garlic, chili powder, cumin, salt, and pepper. Mix until everything is well combined.
Using your hands, form the mixture into 4 evenly sized patties.
Heat the olive oil in a large skillet over medium heat.
Once the oil is hot, add the patties to the skillet and cook for 3-4 minutes on each side, or until they are browned and crispy on the outside.
While the burgers are cooking, toast the buns and prepare any toppings you'd like to add.
Once the burgers are done, assemble them on the toasted buns with your desired toppings.
Serve hot and enjoy your delicious veggie burgers!

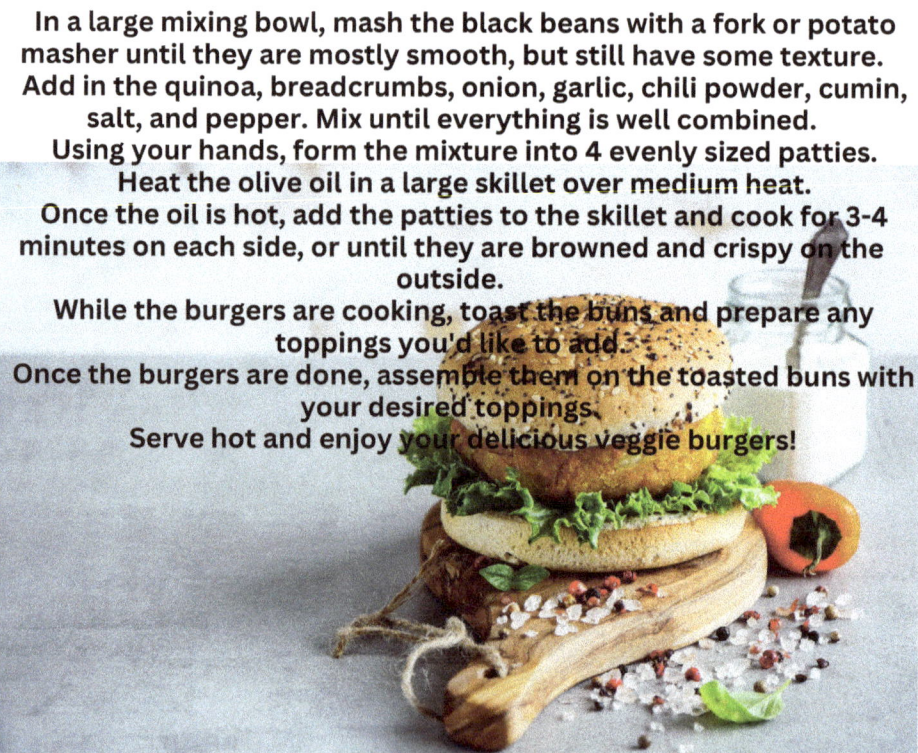

# Macro Veggie Bowl

Ingredients:

1 cup quinoa
1 sweet potato, cubed
1 red bell pepper, sliced
1 yellow bell pepper, sliced
1 zucchini, sliced
1 cup broccoli florets
1 avocado, sliced
1/4 cup pumpkin seeds
1/4 cup sunflower seeds
1/4 cup chopped fresh parsley
Salt and pepper, to taste
Olive oil, for roasting

For the dressing:

1/4 cup tahini
1/4 cup apple cider vinegar
2 tablespoons honey
1 tablespoon dijon mustard
Juice of 1 lemon
Salt and pepper, to taste
Water, as needed to thin the dressing

**Instructions:**

Preheat the oven to 400°F. Line a baking sheet with parchment paper.
Cook quinoa according to package instructions.
Place sweet potato, red bell pepper, yellow bell pepper, zucchini, and broccoli on the baking sheet. Drizzle with olive oil and season with salt and pepper.
Roast in the oven for 20-25 minutes or until vegetables are tender and lightly browned.
In a small bowl, whisk together tahini, apple cider vinegar, honey, dijon mustard, lemon juice, salt, and pepper. Add water to thin the dressing if needed.
To assemble the bowl, divide cooked quinoa among serving bowls. Top with roasted vegetables, sliced avocado, pumpkin seeds, sunflower seeds, and chopped parsley. Drizzle with the dressing and serve. Enjoy your macro veggie bowl!

# Mushroom Burger

Here's a recipe for a delicious mushroom burger:

Ingredients:

4 portobello mushroom caps
1/4 cup balsamic vinegar
2 tablespoons olive oil
1 teaspoon dried thyme
1/2 teaspoon garlic powder
Salt and black pepper
4 burger buns
Toppings of your choice (lettuce, tomato, onion, etc.)

**Instructions:**

Preheat your grill or grill pan to medium-high heat.
Clean the portobello mushrooms and remove the stems. Use a spoon to gently scrape out the gills and discard them.
In a small bowl, whisk together the balsamic vinegar, olive oil, thyme, garlic powder, salt, and pepper.
Brush the marinade over both sides of the mushroom caps, making sure they are fully coated.
Place the mushrooms on the grill and cook for 4-5 minutes on each side, or until they are tender and juicy.
While the mushrooms are cooking, toast your burger buns on the grill.
Assemble your burgers by placing the cooked mushrooms on the toasted buns and adding your desired toppings.
Serve immediately and enjoy your delicious mushroom burger!

# Crispy Baked Falafel

Here's a recipe for crispy baked falafel:

Ingredients:

2 cups cooked chickpeas, drained and rinsed
1/2 onion, chopped
3 cloves garlic, minced
1/4 cup chopped fresh parsley
1/4 cup chopped fresh cilantro
1 teaspoon ground cumin
1 teaspoon ground coriander
1/2 teaspoon paprika
1/4 teaspoon cayenne pepper
1 teaspoon salt
1/4 teaspoon black pepper
1/4 cup all-purpose flour
1 teaspoon baking powder
2 tablespoons olive oil

**Instructions:**

Preheat the oven to 375°F (190°C) and line a baking sheet with parchment paper.
In a food processor, pulse the chickpeas, onion, garlic, parsley, cilantro, cumin, coriander, paprika, cayenne pepper, salt, and black pepper until the mixture is coarse and crumbly.
Add the flour and baking powder to the food processor and pulse until the mixture forms a dough.
Form the dough into 2-inch balls and flatten slightly to form patties.
Place the patties on the prepared baking sheet and brush each one with olive oil.
Bake for 20-25 minutes, or until the falafel is crispy and golden brown.
Serve the falafel with pita bread, hummus, and your favorite veggies.
Enjoy!

# Chickpea Salald Sandwich

Ingredients:

1 can chickpeas, drained and rinsed
1/4 cup diced red onion
1/4 cup diced celery
2 tbsp chopped fresh parsley
2 tbsp chopped fresh dill
2 tbsp vegan mayo
1 tbsp dijon mustard
1 tbsp fresh lemon juice
Salt and pepper, to taste
Sliced bread or buns of your choice
Lettuce, tomato, or any additional toppings you prefer

Instructions:

Preheat oven to 375°F (190°C).
In a bowl, mash the chickpeas with a fork or potato masher until they're mostly broken up.
Add in the red onion, celery, parsley, and dill, and stir until combined.
In a separate small bowl, mix together the vegan mayo, dijon mustard, lemon juice, salt, and pepper.
Pour the mayo mixture over the chickpea mixture and stir until everything is well-coated.
Line a baking sheet with parchment paper.
Scoop the chickpea salad onto the baking sheet using a spoon or cookie scoop, forming each scoop into a round patty shape.
Bake the chickpea patties for 15-20 minutes, until they're crispy on the outside and warmed through.
Toast your bread or buns, and assemble your sandwich with the chickpea patties, lettuce, tomato, and any other toppings you like.
Enjoy your delicious and protein-packed chickpea salad sandwich!

# Sweet Potato Salad

Ingredients:

2 large sweet potatoes, peeled and cubed
1/2 red onion, diced
1 red bell pepper, diced
1/4 cup chopped fresh cilantro
1/4 cup chopped pecans
2 tablespoons olive oil
2 tablespoons apple cider vinegar
1 tablespoon honey
1 teaspoon Dijon mustard
Salt and black pepper, to taste

Instructions:

Preheat oven to 400°F (200°C).
Spread the sweet potato cubes in a single layer on a baking sheet lined with parchment paper. Drizzle with 1 tablespoon of olive oil and sprinkle with salt and pepper. Toss to coat.
Roast sweet potatoes for 25-30 minutes or until they are tender and golden brown. Remove from the oven and let cool.
In a small bowl, whisk together 1 tablespoon of olive oil, apple cider vinegar, honey, Dijon mustard, salt, and pepper until well combined.
In a large mixing bowl, combine the cooled sweet potatoes, diced red onion, diced red bell pepper, chopped cilantro, and chopped pecans.
Pour the dressing over the sweet potato mixture and toss to coat.
Serve chilled or at room temperature.

This sweet potato salad is perfect for a healthy and flavorful side dish for any meal. Enjoy!

# Mediterranean Stuffed Eggplant

Here's a recipe for a delicious Mediterranean stuffed eggplant:

Ingredients:

2 medium eggplants
1/2 cup uncooked quinoa
1 can chickpeas, drained and rinsed
1/2 cup chopped cherry tomatoes
1/4 cup chopped fresh parsley
1/4 cup chopped fresh mint
1/4 cup chopped Kalamata olives
1/4 cup crumbled feta cheese
1 tablespoon olive oil
2 cloves garlic, minced
Salt and black pepper, to taste

**Instructions:**

Preheat oven to 400°F (200°C).
Cut the eggplants in half lengthwise and scoop out the flesh, leaving about 1/2 inch around the edges. Reserve the scooped-out flesh for later.
Place the eggplant halves on a baking sheet lined with parchment paper, drizzle with olive oil, and sprinkle with salt and pepper. Roast for 20-25 minutes or until they are tender and golden brown.
While the eggplants are roasting, cook the quinoa according to package instructions.
In a large mixing bowl, combine the cooked quinoa, chickpeas, chopped cherry tomatoes, chopped parsley, chopped mint, chopped Kalamata olives, crumbled feta cheese, minced garlic, and the reserved eggplant flesh. Mix well.
Remove the roasted eggplants from the oven and stuff each half with the quinoa mixture.
Return the stuffed eggplants to the oven and bake for an additional 10-15 minutes, or until the filling is heated through and the feta cheese is melted and slightly golden.
Serve hot and enjoy!

This Mediterranean stuffed eggplant is a tasty and healthy meal that's perfect for vegetarians and meat-eaters alike. It's packed with flavor and nutrients, and it's sure to become a family favorite!

# Easy Vegan Noodle

### Ingredients:

8 oz of noodles of your choice (such as spaghetti or udon)
1/2 cup chopped mushrooms
1/2 cup chopped carrots
1/2 cup chopped red bell pepper
1/2 cup chopped green onions
2 cloves garlic, minced
1/4 cup soy sauce
1 tablespoon sesame oil
1 tablespoon rice vinegar
1 tablespoon maple syrup
1 teaspoon ginger paste
1 teaspoon cornstarch
Salt and black pepper, to taste

### Instructions:

Cook the noodles according to the package instructions. Drain and set aside.
In a small bowl, whisk together the soy sauce, sesame oil, rice vinegar, maple syrup, ginger paste, cornstarch, salt, and pepper.
In a large skillet, heat some oil over medium-high heat. Add the chopped mushrooms, carrots, and red bell pepper. Cook for 5-7 minutes or until the vegetables are tender.
Add the minced garlic and cook for an additional minute, stirring constantly.
Add the chopped green onions and the soy sauce mixture to the skillet. Cook for 2-3 minutes or until the sauce thickens.
Add the cooked noodles to the skillet and toss to coat with the sauce.
Serve hot and enjoy!

This vegan noodle dish is quick and easy to make, and it's packed with flavor and nutrients. You can customize the recipe by using your favorite type of noodles and vegetables. It's a great option for a weeknight dinner or a quick lunch.

# Sesame Vegan Sushi

## Ingredients:

2 cups sushi rice
2 1/2 cups water
1/4 cup rice vinegar
1 tablespoon sugar
1 teaspoon salt
4 sheets of nori seaweed
1 avocado, sliced
1/2 cup sliced cucumber
1/2 cup sliced carrots
1/4 cup sliced scallions
1 tablespoon toasted sesame seeds
Soy sauce, wasabi, and pickled ginger for serving

## Instructions:

Rinse the sushi rice in cold water until the water runs clear.
In a medium saucepan, combine the rinsed rice and water. Bring to a boil, then reduce the heat to low, cover, and simmer for 18-20 minutes or until the rice is tender and the water has been absorbed.
In a small bowl, whisk together the rice vinegar, sugar, and salt until the sugar and salt have dissolved.
Once the rice is cooked, transfer it to a large bowl and add the rice vinegar mixture. Stir gently to combine.
Lay a sheet of nori seaweed on a clean surface. Place a small amount of rice on the nori, leaving a 1-inch border at the top edge.
Add a few slices of avocado, cucumber, carrots, and scallions to the center of the rice.
Roll the sushi tightly, using the border of rice at the top edge to seal the roll.
Repeat with the remaining ingredients.
Slice the sushi rolls into bite-size pieces.
Sprinkle toasted sesame seeds over the sushi pieces.
Serve with soy sauce, wasabi, and pickled ginger.

This sesame vegan sushi is a healthy and delicious meal that's perfect for a light lunch or dinner. The combination of fresh vegetables, creamy avocado, and nutty sesame seeds makes for a satisfying and flavorful bite.

# Maki Sushi

Ingredients:

2 cups sushi rice
2 1/2 cups water
1/4 cup rice vinegar
1 tablespoon sugar
1 teaspoon salt
4 sheets of nori seaweed
1/2 cup thinly sliced carrots
1/2 cup thinly sliced cucumber
1/2 cup thinly sliced avocado
1/2 cup thinly sliced red bell pepper
1/4 cup sliced scallions
Soy sauce, wasabi, and pickled ginger for serving

Instructions:

Rinse the sushi rice in cold water until the water runs clear.
In a medium saucepan, combine the rinsed rice and water. Bring to a boil, then reduce the heat to low, cover, and simmer for 18-20 minutes or until the rice is tender and the water has been absorbed.
In a small bowl, whisk together the rice vinegar, sugar, and salt until the sugar and salt have dissolved.
Once the rice is cooked, transfer it to a large bowl and add the rice vinegar mixture. Stir gently to combine.
Lay a sheet of nori seaweed on a clean surface, shiny side down.
Wet your hands with water and take a small amount of rice, about the size of a golf ball, and spread it evenly over the nori, leaving a 1-inch border at the top edge.
Add a few slices of carrots, cucumber, avocado, red bell pepper, and scallions to the center of the rice.
Using the border of rice at the top edge as a guide, roll the sushi tightly.
Repeat with the remaining ingredients.
Slice the sushi rolls into bite-size pieces.
Serve with soy sauce, wasabi, and pickled ginger.

This vegan maki sushi is a healthy and delicious meal that's perfect for a light lunch or dinner. The combination of fresh vegetables and creamy avocado makes for a satisfying and flavorful bite. You can customize the recipe by using your favorite vegetables or adding a protein such as tofu or tempeh.

# Noodles With Cashew Coconut Sauce

Ingredients:

8 oz. of noodles (your choice of pasta, rice noodles, or soba noodles)
1/2 cup raw cashews
1/2 cup coconut milk
2 tablespoons soy sauce
2 tablespoons rice vinegar
2 tablespoons maple syrup
1 tablespoon sriracha (optional)
1 tablespoon grated ginger
2 garlic cloves, minced
2 green onions, sliced (optional)
2 tablespoons chopped cilantro (optional)
1 tablespoon coconut oil or vegetable oil

Instructions:

Cook noodles according to package instructions until al dente. Drain and set aside.
In a blender or food processor, blend the cashews, coconut milk, soy sauce, rice vinegar, maple syrup, sriracha, ginger, and garlic until smooth and creamy.
In a large skillet or wok, heat the coconut oil over medium heat.
Add the cashew coconut sauce to the skillet and cook for 2-3 minutes, stirring constantly.
Add the cooked noodles to the skillet and toss to coat in the sauce.
Cook for an additional 2-3 minutes until the noodles are heated through.
Garnish with sliced green onions and chopped cilantro (if using).
Serve hot and enjoy!
This noodles with cashew coconut sauce recipe is a vegan, gluten-free, and dairy-free alternative to traditional pasta dishes. The cashew coconut sauce adds a creamy and nutty flavor that complements the noodles perfectly. You can also add your favorite veggies like broccoli, bell peppers, or snap peas to make it more colorful and nutritious.

# Radish Salad

Ingredients:

1 bunch of radishes, thinly sliced
1/2 red onion, thinly sliced
1/4 cup chopped fresh parsley
1/4 cup chopped fresh mint
1/4 cup chopped fresh cilantro
1/4 cup olive oil
2 tablespoons white wine vinegar
1 tablespoon honey (or agave syrup for a vegan option)
1 teaspoon Dijon mustard
Salt and pepper to taste

Instructions:

In a large bowl, combine the sliced radishes and red onion.
In a small bowl, whisk together the olive oil, white wine vinegar, honey, Dijon mustard, and salt and pepper until well combined.
Pour the dressing over the radish and onion mixture, and toss to coat.
Add the chopped parsley, mint, and cilantro to the bowl, and toss again to combine.
Adjust seasoning as needed.
Let the salad sit for at least 10-15 minutes to allow the flavors to meld together.
Serve and enjoy!
This radish salad is a great side dish or a light lunch option. The combination of fresh herbs and tangy dressing pairs perfectly with the crunchy texture of the radishes. You can also add some crumbled feta cheese or toasted almonds for some extra flavor and crunch.

# Kale Salad With Ginger Dressing

Ingredients:

1 bunch of kale, stems removed and leaves torn into bite-sized pieces
1 red bell pepper, thinly sliced
1 carrot, peeled and julienned
1/4 cup sliced almonds, toasted
2 tablespoons sesame seeds, toasted
1 tablespoon grated fresh ginger
1 garlic clove, minced
2 tablespoons rice vinegar
2 tablespoons soy sauce
1 tablespoon honey (or maple syrup for a vegan option)
1/4 cup olive oil
Salt and pepper to taste

Instructions:

In a large bowl, combine the kale, red bell pepper, and carrot.
In a small bowl, whisk together the grated ginger, minced garlic, rice vinegar, soy sauce, honey, olive oil, salt, and pepper until well combined.
Pour the dressing over the kale mixture, and toss to coat.
Let the salad sit for at least 10-15 minutes to allow the kale to wilt slightly and absorb the flavors.
Add the sliced almonds and toasted sesame seeds to the salad, and toss again to combine.
Serve and enjoy!

This kale salad with ginger dressing is a flavorful and nutritious option for any meal. The ginger and garlic add a zesty kick to the salad, while the toasted almonds and sesame seeds provide some crunch. You can also add some grilled chicken or tofu for some extra protein, or some sliced avocado for some healthy fats.

# Roasted Cauliflower Salad

Ingredients:

1 head of cauliflower, chopped into small florets
1 red onion, thinly sliced
1 can of chickpeas, drained and rinsed
2 tablespoons olive oil
1 teaspoon smoked paprika
Salt and pepper to taste
2 cups mixed greens
1/4 cup chopped fresh parsley
1/4 cup crumbled feta cheese (optional)

For the dressing:

1/4 cup olive oil
2 tablespoons red wine vinegar
1 tablespoon honey (or agave syrup for a vegan option)
1 teaspoon Dijon mustard
1 garlic clove, minced
Salt and pepper to taste

Instructions:

Preheat the oven to 400°F.
In a large bowl, toss the cauliflower florets, sliced red onion, and chickpeas with the olive oil, smoked paprika, salt, and pepper until well coated.
Spread the mixture out on a baking sheet in a single layer, and roast in the oven for 25-30 minutes until the cauliflower is tender and lightly browned.
While the cauliflower is roasting, prepare the dressing by whisking together the olive oil, red wine vinegar, honey, Dijon mustard, minced garlic, salt, and pepper in a small bowl.
Once the cauliflower is done, remove it from the oven and let it cool slightly.
In a large bowl, combine the roasted cauliflower mixture, mixed greens, and chopped parsley.
Drizzle the dressing over the salad, and toss to coat.
If desired, sprinkle crumbled feta cheese over the top of the salad.
Serve warm or at room temperature, and enjoy!

This roasted cauliflower salad is a healthy and flavorful way to enjoy this nutritious vegetable. The combination of smoky paprika, sweet roasted onions, and tender cauliflower is complemented by the tangy dressing and fresh greens. You can also add some toasted almonds or sunflower seeds for some extra crunch and protein.

# Healthy Taco Salad

Ingredients:
For the salad:

1 head of romaine lettuce, chopped
1 can of black beans, drained and rinsed
1 red bell pepper, chopped
1 avocado, diced
1/2 cup fresh cilantro, chopped
1/4 cup green onions, sliced
1/2 cup tortilla chips, crushed

For the taco seasoning:

1 tablespoon chili powder
1 teaspoon ground cumin
1/2 teaspoon paprika
1/4 teaspoon garlic powder
1/4 teaspoon onion powder
1/4 teaspoon dried oregano
1/4 teaspoon salt
1/4 teaspoon black pepper

For the dressing:

1/4 cup vegan sour cream
2 tablespoons fresh lime juice
1 tablespoon chopped fresh cilantro
1/4 teaspoon garlic powder
Salt and pepper to taste

Instructions:

In a small bowl, whisk together the taco seasoning ingredients.
In a large skillet over medium-high heat, add the black beans and the taco seasoning, and cook for 5-7 minutes until heated through and well-coated.
In a large bowl, combine the chopped romaine lettuce, red bell pepper, diced avocado, chopped cilantro, and sliced green onions.
Add the warm seasoned black beans to the bowl, and toss to combine.
In a small bowl, whisk together the vegan sour cream, fresh lime juice, chopped cilantro, garlic powder, salt, and pepper to make the dressing.
Drizzle the dressing over the salad, and toss to coat.
Sprinkle the crushed tortilla chips over the top of the salad.
Serve and enjoy!
This vegan taco salad is a flavorful and healthy option for any meal. The combination of crunchy vegetables, seasoned black beans, and zesty dressing is sure to satisfy your taste buds. You can also add some diced tomatoes, sliced jalapeños, or vegan cheese for some extra flavor and texture.

# Butternut Squash Soup

Here is a recipe for a comforting and delicious vegan butternut squash soup:

Ingredients:

1 medium butternut squash, peeled and chopped into cubes
1 onion, chopped
2 cloves of garlic, minced
1 tablespoon olive oil
4 cups vegetable broth
1 teaspoon ground cinnamon
1/4 teaspoon ground nutmeg
Salt and pepper to taste
1/2 cup coconut milk
2 tablespoons maple syrup

Instructions:

Preheat your oven to 400°F.
Place the chopped butternut squash on a baking sheet, drizzle with olive oil, and sprinkle with salt and pepper.
Roast the butternut squash in the oven for about 30 minutes, or until tender and lightly browned.
In a large pot, heat the olive oil over medium heat.
Add the chopped onion and minced garlic to the pot and sauté until soft and translucent.
Add the roasted butternut squash to the pot and stir well to combine with the onions and garlic.
Add the vegetable broth, ground cinnamon, ground nutmeg, salt, and pepper to the pot and bring to a boil.
Reduce the heat to low and let the soup simmer for about 15 minutes.
Use an immersion blender or transfer the soup to a blender and blend until smooth and creamy.
Stir in the coconut milk and maple syrup.
Adjust the seasoning to taste, adding more salt, pepper, cinnamon or nutmeg as needed.
Serve hot with crusty bread or crackers on top, and enjoy!

This vegan butternut squash soup is a comforting and healthy option for any meal. The combination of the roasted butternut squash, warming spices, and creamy coconut milk is perfect for a chilly day. You can also add some roasted pumpkin seeds or croutons on top for extra texture and flavor.

# Delicious Broccoli Soup

Ingredients:

1 head of broccoli, chopped into florets
1 onion, chopped
2 cloves of garlic, minced
1 tablespoon olive oil
4 cups vegetable broth
1/2 teaspoon ground cumin
1/4 teaspoon ground turmeric
Salt and pepper to taste
1/2 cup coconut milk
2 tablespoons nutritional yeast (optional)

Instructions:

In a large pot, heat the olive oil over medium heat.
Add the chopped onion and minced garlic to the pot and sauté until soft and translucent.
Add the chopped broccoli to the pot and stir well to combine with the onions and garlic.
Add the vegetable broth, ground cumin, ground turmeric, salt, and pepper to the pot and bring to a boil.
Reduce the heat to low and let the soup simmer for about 20 minutes, or until the broccoli is tender.
Use an immersion blender or transfer the soup to a blender and blend until smooth and creamy.
Stir in the coconut milk and nutritional yeast (if using).
Adjust the seasoning to taste, adding more salt, pepper, cumin, or turmeric as needed.
Serve hot with crusty bread or crackers on top, and enjoy!

# Best Lentil Soup

Ingredients:

1 cup dried lentils
1 onion, chopped
2 cloves garlic, minced
2 carrots, peeled and chopped
2 celery stalks, chopped
1 tablespoon olive oil
4 cups vegetable broth
1 teaspoon ground cumin
1 teaspoon dried thyme
Salt and pepper, to taste
Lemon wedges, for serving

Instructions:

Rinse the lentils and soak them in water for at least an hour. Drain and set aside.
Heat the olive oil in a large pot over medium heat. Add the onion and garlic and cook until softened.

Add the carrots and celery and cook for a few more minutes until they start to soften.
Add the lentils, vegetable broth, cumin, thyme, salt, and pepper.
Bring to a boil, then reduce heat and simmer for 30-40 minutes, or until the lentils are tender.
Use an immersion blender or transfer the soup to a blender and blend until smooth.
Serve the soup with a squeeze of fresh lemon juice and crusty bread.
Enjoy your warm and hearty lentil soup!

# Easy Coconut Curry

Ingredients:

1 tablespoon coconut oil
1 medium onion, chopped
3 garlic cloves, minced
1 tablespoon fresh ginger, minced
1 tablespoon curry powder
1 teaspoon ground turmeric
1 teaspoon ground cumin
1 teaspoon ground coriander
1 can of chickpeas, drained and rinsed
2 cups chopped vegetables (such as bell peppers, zucchini, and carrots)
1 can of coconut milk
1 tablespoon soy sauce or tamari
1 tablespoon maple syrup
1 tablespoon lime juice
Salt and pepper to taste
Cooked rice or quinoa, for serving
Chopped cilantro, for garnish

Instructions:

In a large pot or Dutch oven, heat the coconut oil over medium heat.
Add the onion and cook for 5-7 minutes until softened and translucent.
Add the garlic and ginger and cook for 1-2 minutes until fragrant.
Add the curry powder, turmeric, cumin, and coriander and cook for another minute until the spices are toasted and fragrant.
Add the chickpeas and chopped vegetables and stir to combine.
Pour in the can of coconut milk and stir to combine.
Add the soy sauce or tamari, maple syrup, and lime juice and stir to combine.
Bring the curry to a simmer and cook for 15-20 minutes until the vegetables are tender.
Season with salt and pepper to taste.
Serve the curry over cooked rice or quinoa and garnish with chopped cilantro.
Enjoy your vegan coconut curry!

# Vegetarian Chilli

Ingredients:

2 tablespoons olive oil
1 large onion, chopped
3 garlic cloves, minced
2 bell peppers, chopped
2 tablespoons chili powder
1 tablespoon ground cumin
1 teaspoon smoked paprika
1/2 teaspoon dried oregano
1/2 teaspoon salt
1/4 teaspoon black pepper
2 cans of kidney beans, drained and rinsed
1 can of diced tomatoes
1 cup of corn kernels
1 cup of vegetable broth
1 tablespoon soy sauce or tamari
1 tablespoon lime juice
Optional toppings: shredded cheese, chopped cilantro, sour cream or Greek yogurt, avocado

Instructions:

In a large pot or Dutch oven, heat the olive oil over medium heat.
Add the onion and garlic and cook for 5-7 minutes until softened and translucent.
Add the bell peppers and cook for another 5 minutes until softened.
Add the chili powder, cumin, smoked paprika, oregano, salt, and black pepper and stir to combine.
Add the kidney beans, diced tomatoes (with juice), corn, and vegetable broth and stir to combine.
Bring the chili to a simmer and cook for 20-25 minutes until the flavors have melded together and the chili has thickened.
Add the soy sauce or tamari and lime juice and stir to combine.
Serve the chili hot with your favorite toppings, such as shredded cheese, chopped cilantro, sour cream or Greek yogurt, or avocado.
Enjoy your vegetarian chili! It's a hearty and healthy meal that's perfect for a cozy night in.

# Tomato Basil Soup

Ingredients:

2 tablespoons olive oil
1 large onion, chopped
3 garlic cloves, minced
2 cans of whole peeled tomatoes
2 cups of vegetable broth
1/4 cup of fresh basil leaves, chopped
1/2 cup of heavy cream (optional)
Salt and pepper to taste
Croutons or bread for serving (optional)

Instructions:

In a large pot or Dutch oven, heat the olive oil over medium heat.
Add the onion and garlic and cook for 5-7 minutes until softened and translucent.
Add the cans of whole peeled tomatoes (with their juice) and stir to combine.
Add the vegetable broth and bring the mixture to a simmer.
Cook for 15-20 minutes until the tomatoes have broken down and the flavors have melded together.
Add the chopped basil leaves and stir to combine.
Using an immersion blender or working in batches with a regular blender, puree the soup until smooth.
Return the soup to the pot and add the heavy cream (if using). Stir to combine.
Season with salt and pepper to taste.
Serve the soup hot with croutons or bread for dipping, if desired.
Enjoy your tomato basil soup! It's a comforting and classic dish that's perfect for any time of year.

# Mushroom Soup

Ingredients:

2 tablespoons olive oil
1 onion, chopped
3 garlic cloves, minced
1 lb mushrooms (such as button or cremini), sliced
4 cups vegetable broth
1 cup unsweetened almond milk or coconut milk
2 tablespoons nutritional yeast (optional)
1/2 teaspoon dried thyme
1/2 teaspoon dried rosemary
Salt and pepper, to taste
Chopped fresh parsley, for garnish

Instructions:

In a large pot or Dutch oven, heat the olive oil over medium heat. Add the chopped onion and garlic, and sauté for about 5 minutes, until the onions are soft and translucent.
Add the sliced mushrooms and sauté for about 8-10 minutes until the mushrooms have released their liquid and are tender.
Add the vegetable broth, almond milk, nutritional yeast (if using), thyme, and rosemary, and bring the soup to a simmer.
Allow the soup to simmer for about 10-15 minutes to allow the flavors to meld together.
Use an immersion blender to blend the soup until it is smooth and creamy. If you don't have an immersion blender, you can carefully transfer the soup to a blender in batches and blend until smooth.
Return the soup to the pot and season with salt and pepper to taste.
Serve hot, garnished with chopped parsley.
Enjoy your delicious vegan mushroom soup! It's a hearty and satisfying dish that's perfect for a cozy night in.

# Bolognese Pasta

Ingredients:

1 pound of spaghetti or pasta of your choice
1 large onion, chopped
3 garlic cloves, minced
2 carrots, finely chopped
2 celery stalks, finely chopped
1 red bell pepper, chopped
1 can (28 ounces) of crushed tomatoes
1 can (15 ounces) of tomato sauce
1 tablespoon of tomato paste
1 teaspoon of dried oregano
1 teaspoon of dried basil
1 teaspoon of dried thyme
1 teaspoon of salt
1/2 teaspoon of black pepper
2 tablespoons of olive oil
1/4 cup of chopped fresh parsley
Vegan Parmesan cheese for serving (optional)

Instructions:

Cook the pasta according to package instructions until al dente. Drain the pasta and set it aside.
In a large pot or Dutch oven, heat the olive oil over medium-high heat. Add the onion and sauté for 3-4 minutes, or until the onion is translucent.
Add the garlic, carrots, celery, and red bell pepper to the pot. Cook for 5-7 minutes or until the vegetables are tender.
Add the crushed tomatoes, tomato sauce, tomato paste, dried oregano, dried basil, dried thyme, salt, and black peper to the pot. Stir well to combine.
Bring the sauce to a boil, then reduce the heat to low and let it simmer for 20-25 minutes, stirring occasionally.
Once the sauce has thickened and the vegetables are tender, add the chopped fresh parsley and stir well.
Serve the sauce over the cooked pasta and top with vegan Parmesan cheese (if using). Enjoy your delicious vegan bolognese pasta!

# Vegan Burritos

Ingredients:

For the filling:

1 can (15 ounces) of black beans, drained and rinsed
1 cup of cooked brown rice
1 red bell pepper, chopped
1 yellow onion, chopped
1 teaspoon of chili powder
1 teaspoon of cumin
1/2 teaspoon of smoked paprika
Salt and pepper to taste
2 tablespoons of olive oil

For the burritos:

6-8 large flour tortillas
1 avocado, sliced
1/4 cup of chopped fresh cilantro
1 lime, cut into wedges
Vegan sour cream for serving (optional)

Instructions:

Heat the olive oil in a large skillet over medium-high heat. Add the red bell pepper and onion and cook for 5-7 minutes or until the vegetables are tender.
Add the black beans, cooked brown rice, chili powder, cumin, smoked paprika, salt, and pepper to the skillet. Stir well to combine and cook for an additional 2-3 minutes to heat through.
Warm the flour tortillas in the microwave or on a skillet until they are soft and pliable.
Assemble the burritos by placing a spoonful of the black bean and rice filling in the center of each tortilla. Add a few slices of avocado and a sprinkle of fresh cilantro on top.
Roll the burrito by folding the sides of the tortilla towards the center, then rolling it tightly from the bottom up.
Serve the burritos with lime wedges and vegan sour cream (if using).
Enjoy your delicious vegan burritos!

# Coconut Rice Bowl

Ingredients:

For the coconut rice:

1 cup of jasmine rice
1 can (14 ounces) of coconut milk
1/2 cup of water
1/4 teaspoon of salt

For the toppings:

1 avocado, sliced
1/2 cup of sliced cucumbers
1/2 cup of shredded carrots
1/2 cup of edamame
1/4 cup of chopped fresh cilantro
1 lime, cut into wedges
Sriracha or hot sauce (optional)

Instructions:

Rinse the jasmine rice in cold water until the water runs clear.
In a medium-sized saucepan, combine the rinsed rice, coconut milk, water, and salt. Stir well to combine.
Bring the rice mixture to a boil, then reduce the heat to low and cover the saucepan with a lid. Let the rice cook for 18-20 minutes, or until all the liquid has been absorbed.
Once the rice is cooked, fluff it with a fork and set it aside.
To assemble the coconut rice bowl, divide the cooked rice into bowls. Top each bowl with sliced avocado, sliced cucumbers, shredded carrots, and edamame.
Sprinkle fresh cilantro on top of each bowl and add a lime wedge.
Add sriracha or hot sauce (if using) for a spicy kick.
Enjoy your delicious and nourishing coconut rice bowl!

# Vegetable Biryani

For the biryani:

2 tablespoons of vegetable oil
1 onion, chopped
1 teaspoon of ginger paste
1 teaspoon of garlic paste
1 teaspoon of cumin seeds
1 teaspoon of coriander powder
1 teaspoon of garam masala
1/2 teaspoon of turmeric powder
1/2 teaspoon of red chili powder (optional)
2 cups of mixed vegetables (such as carrots, peas, potatoes, and green beans)
Salt to taste
1/4 cup of chopped fresh cilantro
1/4 cup of chopped fresh mint
1/2 cup of toasted cashews (optional)

Ingredients:

For the rice:

2 cups of basmati rice
4 cups of water
1 cinnamon stick
3-4 green cardamom pods
3-4 cloves
1 bay leaf
Salt to taste

Instructions:

Rinse the basmati rice in cold water until the water runs clear. Soak the rice in water for 20 minutes.
In a large pot, bring the 4 cups of water to a boil. Add the soaked rice, cinnamon stick, green cardamom pods, cloves, bay leaf, and salt to the pot. Stir well to combine.
Reduce the heat to low, cover the pot with a lid, and let the rice cook for 15-20 minutes, or until all the water has been absorbed and the rice is fully cooked.
Once the rice is cooked, remove the whole spices and fluff the rice with a fork. Set the rice aside.
In a large skillet, heat the vegetable oil over medium-high heat. Add the chopped onion and sauté for 2-3 minutes or until the onion is translucent.
Add the ginger paste, garlic paste, and cumin seeds to the skillet. Cook for 1-2 minutes, stirring constantly.
Add the coriander powder, garam masala, turmeric powder, and red chili powder (if using) to the skillet. Stir well to combine.
Add the mixed vegetables to the skillet and cook for 5-7 minutes or until the vegetables are tender. Season the vegetable mixture with salt to taste.
In a large bowl, combine the cooked rice, vegetable mixture, chopped fresh cilantro, chopped fresh mint, and toasted cashews (if using). Stir well to combine.
Transfer the biryani mixture to a serving dish and garnish with additional cilantro and mint.
Serve hot and enjoy your delicious vegetable biryani!

# Crispy Tofu Sandwich

Ingredients:

For the crispy tofu:

1 block (14-16 oz) of extra firm tofu
1/4 cup of cornstarch
1/4 cup of all-purpose flour
1 teaspoon of garlic powder
1/2 teaspoon of salt
1/4 teaspoon of black pepper
1/4 cup of vegetable oil

For the sandwich:

4 slices of bread
4 lettuce leaves
1 tomato, sliced
1/2 avocado, sliced
Vegan mayonnaise or your favorite spread

Instructions:

Drain the block of extra firm tofu and pat it dry with paper towels.
Cut the tofu into 1/2-inch slices and place them on a plate lined with paper towels. Cover the tofu slices with more paper towels and press down gently to remove any excess moisture
In a shallow dish, whisk together the cornstarch, all-purpose flour, garlic powder, salt, and black pepper.
Dredge each tofu slice in the flour mixture, shaking off any excess.
In a large skillet, heat the vegetable oil over medium-high heat.
Add the coated tofu slices to the skillet and cook for 3-4 minutes on each side, or until the tofu is crispy and golden brown.
Once the tofu is cooked, transfer it to a plate lined with paper towels to remove any excess oil.
To assemble the sandwich, toast the bread slices and spread vegan mayonnaise or your favorite spread on each slice.
Add a lettuce leaf to each slice of bread, followed by sliced tomato and sliced avocado.
Add 2-3 slices of crispy tofu on top of the avocado.
Top the sandwich with the remaining bread slice.
Cut the sandwich in half and serve hot.
Enjoy your delicious and satisfying crispy tofu sandwich!

# Roasted Cauliflower

Roasted cauliflower is a simple and delicious side dish that's perfect for any meal. Here's a recipe that's easy to follow and yields a crispy and flavorful result:

Ingredients:

1 head of cauliflower, cut into bite-sized florets
3 tablespoons olive oil
1 teaspoon salt
1/2 teaspoon black pepper
1/2 teaspoon garlic powder
1/2 teaspoon paprika

Instructions:

Preheat your oven to 425°F (218°C) and line a baking sheet with parchment paper.
In a large mixing bowl, toss the cauliflower florets with olive oil, salt, pepper, garlic powder, and paprika until they are evenly coated.
Spread the cauliflower in a single layer on the prepared baking sheet, making sure not to overcrowd the pan. This will help the cauliflower to roast evenly and become crispy.
Place the baking sheet in the preheated oven and roast the cauliflower for 20-25 minutes or until it is golden brown and crispy on the outside.
Use a spatula to flip the cauliflower halfway through the cooking time to ensure even roasting.
Once the cauliflower is cooked to your desired level of crispiness, remove it from the oven and transfer it to a serving dish.
Garnish with fresh parsley or your favorite herbs, and serve hot.
Enjoy your delicious roasted cauliflower as a side dish or snack. It pairs well with grilled meats, roasted chicken, or can be enjoyed on its own as a healthy and flavorful snack.

# Portobello Mushroom Tacos

If you're looking for a tasty and satisfying vegan meal, try these delicious portobello mushroom tacos. This recipe is quick and easy to prepare, and packed with flavor and nutrients.

Ingredients:

4 large portobello mushrooms, cleaned and sliced
1 tablespoon olive oil
1 tablespoon soy sauce or tamari
1 teaspoon chili powder
1/2 teaspoon ground cumin
1/2 teaspoon smoked paprika
1/4 teaspoon garlic powder
Salt and pepper, to taste
8 small corn tortillas
1 cup shredded lettuce
1/2 cup diced tomatoes
1/2 cup diced red onion
1/4 cup chopped fresh cilantro
Lime wedges, for serving

Instructions:

In a large mixing bowl, combine the sliced mushrooms, olive oil, soy sauce or tamari, chili powder, cumin, smoked paprika, garlic powder, salt, and pepper. Toss until the mushrooms are evenly coated.
Heat a large skillet over medium-high heat. Add the seasoned mushrooms to the skillet and cook for 5-7 minutes, stirring occasionally, until the mushrooms are tender and slightly charred.
While the mushrooms are cooking, warm the tortillas on a separate skillet over medium heat for 1-2 minutes on each side.
To assemble the tacos, place a few slices of the cooked mushrooms on each tortilla. Top with shredded lettuce, diced tomatoes, red onion, and cilantro. Squeeze fresh lime juice over the top.
Serve hot and enjoy!
These vegan portobello tacos are a great way to enjoy a meatless meal that's both satisfying and flavorful. They are also a great option for a quick and easy weeknight dinner or a fun and casual weekend lunch.

# Vegan Shepherds Pie

Vegan shepherd's pie is a classic comfort food dish that is hearty, filling, and full of flavor. This recipe is made with nutritious plant-based ingredients and is sure to be a hit with vegans and meat-eaters alike.

Ingredients:

For the filling:

1 tablespoon olive oil
1 large onion, chopped
2 garlic cloves, minced
2 medium carrots, peeled and chopped
2 celery stalks, chopped
1 cup sliced mushrooms
1 cup cooked lentils
1 cup vegetable broth
1 tablespoon tomato paste
1 tablespoon soy sauce or tamari
1 tablespoon flour
1/2 teaspoon dried thyme
Salt and pepper, to taste

For the mashed potato topping:

2 pounds potatoes, peeled and chopped
2 tablespoons vegan butter or olive oil
1/4 cup non-dairy milk
Salt and pepper, to taste

Instructions:

Preheat your oven to 375°F (190°C).

To make the filling, heat the olive oil in a large skillet over medium heat. Add the onion and garlic and sauté for 2-3 minutes until fragrant.
Add the chopped carrots, celery, and mushrooms and sauté for 5-7 minutes until the vegetables are tender.
Add the cooked lentils, vegetable broth, tomato paste, soy sauce or tamari, flour, dried thyme, salt, and pepper. Stir well to combine.
Bring the mixture to a simmer and cook for 5-7 minutes until the sauce has thickened.
Transfer the filling to a 9x13 inch baking dish.
To make the mashed potato topping, boil the potatoes in a large pot of salted water for 15-20 minutes until they are tender. Drain the potatoes and return them to the pot.
Add the vegan butter or olive oil, non-dairy milk, salt, and pepper to the pot with the potatoes. Mash the potatoes until they are smooth and creamy.
Spread the mashed potatoes over the top of the filling in the baking dish.
Bake the vegan shepherd's pie in the preheated oven for 25-30 minutes until the top is golden brown and crispy.
Serve hot and enjoy!
This vegan shepherd's pie is a comforting and satisfying meal that's perfect for chilly nights or for feeding a crowd. It's packed with plant-based protein and fiber, and it's also a great way to use up leftover mashed potatoes or cooked lentils.

# Spicy Eggplant Sauce

Ingredients:

1 large eggplant, peeled and diced into small pieces
2 tbsp olive oil
1 small onion, finely chopped
3 cloves garlic, minced
1 tbsp tomato paste
1 tsp ground cumin
1 tsp smoked paprika
1/2 tsp cayenne pepper
1/2 tsp salt
1/4 cup water
1 tbsp lemon juice
Chopped fresh parsley or cilantro, for garnish

Instructions:

Heat the olive oil in a large skillet over medium-high heat. Add the diced eggplant and sauté until it's soft and lightly browned, stirring occasionally, about 10-15 minutes.
Add the chopped onion and minced garlic to the skillet and sauté for another 3-4 minutes, or until the onion is soft and translucent.
Stir in the tomato paste, ground cumin, smoked paprika, cayenne pepper, and salt. Cook for another 2-3 minutes, stirring occasionally.
Add the water and lemon juice to the skillet and stir to combine. Reduce the heat to low and let the sauce simmer for 5-10 minutes, or until it's thickened to your liking.
Remove the skillet from the heat and let the sauce cool slightly. Transfer it to a blender or food processor and puree until it's smooth.
Serve the sauce warm or at room temperature, garnished with chopped fresh parsley or cilantro, if desired. This sauce can be used as a dip for vegetables or pita bread, or as a topping for roasted vegetables, rice bowls, or grilled tofu. Enjoy!

# Vegan Alfredo Pasta

Ingredients:

12 oz (340 g) of fettuccine pasta
1 1/2 cups (360 ml) of unsweetened almond milk
1/2 cup (120 ml) of vegetable broth
1/2 cup (60 g) of nutritional yeast
3 cloves of garlic, minced
2 tbsp (30 ml) of olive oil
2 tbsp (30 ml) of cornstarch
1 tsp (5 ml) of salt
1/4 tsp (1.25 ml) of black pepper
Fresh parsley or basil, chopped, for garnish

Instructions:

Cook the fettuccine pasta according to the package instructions until al dente. Drain and set aside.
In a small bowl, whisk together the almond milk, vegetable broth, nutritional yeast, cornstarch, salt, and black pepper.
In a large skillet, heat the olive oil over medium heat. Add the minced garlic and sauté for 1-2 minutes, or until fragrant.
Pour the almond milk mixture into the skillet with the garlic and whisk continuously for 3-5 minutes, or until the sauce starts to thicken.
Add the cooked fettuccine to the skillet with the sauce and toss until the pasta is fully coated in the sauce.
Continue to cook the pasta and sauce for 2-3 minutes, or until the sauce has thickened and the pasta is heated through.
Divide the pasta alfredo into bowls and garnish with chopped fresh parsley or basil.
Enjoy your delicious vegan pasta alfredo!

# Vegan Tikka Masala

**Ingredients:**

For the Tofu Tikka:

14 oz (400 g) block of extra-firm tofu, drained and pressed
1/2 cup (120 ml) of vegan yogurt
2 tbsp (30 ml) of olive oil
2 cloves of garlic, minced
1 tsp (5 ml) of ground cumin
1 tsp (5 ml) of ground coriander
1/2 tsp (2.5 ml) of turmeric
1/2 tsp (2.5 ml) of paprika
Salt and black pepper, to taste

For the Tikka Masala Sauce:

2 tbsp (30 ml) of olive oil
1 small onion, chopped
2 cloves of garlic, minced
1 tbsp (15 ml) of grated ginger
1 tbsp (15 ml) of tomato paste
1 can (14 oz or 400 g) of crushed tomatoes
1 cup (240 ml) of vegetable broth
1 tsp (5 ml) of ground cumin
1 tsp (5 ml) of ground coriander
1/2 tsp (2.5 ml) of turmeric
1/2 tsp (2.5 ml) of smoked paprika
Salt and black pepper, to taste
1/2 cup (120 ml) of vegan cream or full-fat coconut milk
Fresh cilantro, chopped, for garnish

**Instructions:**

To make the tofu tikka, cut the pressed tofu into bite-sized cubes and place them in a large bowl.
In a separate bowl, whisk together the vegan yogurt, olive oil, minced garlic, ground cumin, ground coriander, turmeric, paprika, salt, and black pepper. Pour the marinade over the tofu cubes and toss until the tofu is fully coated.
Preheat the oven to 400°F (200°C) and line a baking sheet with parchment paper. Spread the marinated tofu cubes in a single layer on the baking sheet and bake for 25-30 minutes, or until the tofu is golden brown and crispy.
While the tofu is baking, prepare the tikka masala sauce. In a large skillet, heat the olive oil over medium heat. Add the chopped onion and sauté for 2-3 minutes, or until it's soft and translucent. Add the minced garlic and grated ginger and sauté for another 1-2 minutes.
Stir in the tomato paste, crushed tomatoes, vegetable broth, ground cumin, ground coriander, turmeric, smoked paprika, salt, and black pepper. Bring the sauce to a simmer and let it cook for 10-15 minutes, stirring occasionally.
Once the tofu is done baking, add it to the skillet with the tikka masala sauce. Pour in the vegan cream or full-fat coconut milk and stir until everything is well combined.
Let the sauce and tofu cook together for another 5-10 minutes, or until the sauce has thickened to your liking.
Serve the vegan tikka masala over rice, garnished with chopped fresh cilantro. Enjoy!
Note: If you prefer a smoother sauce, you can puree it in a blender or food processor before adding the tofu.

# Vegan Lentil Meatballs

Ingredients:

1 cup (200 g) of dried brown lentils, rinsed and drained
2 cups (480 ml) of vegetable broth
1 small onion, chopped
3 cloves of garlic, minced
2 tbsp (30 ml) of olive oil
1/2 cup (60 g) of bread crumbs
1/4 cup (30 g) of nutritional yeast
1 tbsp (15 ml) of tomato paste
1 tbsp (15 ml) of soy sauce or tamari
1 tsp (5 ml) of dried oregano
1 tsp (5 ml) of dried basil
Salt and black pepper, to taste

Instructions:

In a medium saucepan, combine the rinsed lentils and vegetable broth. Bring the mixture to a boil over high heat, then reduce the heat to low and simmer, covered, for 25-30 minutes, or until the lentils are soft and most of the liquid has been absorbed. Drain off any excess liquid and let the lentils cool.
Preheat the oven to 400°F (200°C) and line a baking sheet with parchment paper.
In a large skillet, heat the olive oil over medium heat. Add the chopped onion and sauté for 2-3 minutes, or until it's soft and translucent. Add the minced garlic and sauté for another 1-2 minutes.
In a large bowl, combine the cooked lentils, sautéed onion and garlic, bread crumbs, nutritional yeast, tomato paste, soy sauce or tamari, dried oregano, dried basil, salt, and black pepper. Mix everything together until well combined.
Using your hands, form the lentil mixture into golf ball-sized balls and place them on the prepared baking sheet. Bake the lentil meatballs for 20-25 minutes, or until they're golden brown and crispy on the outside.
Serve the vegan lentil meatballs with your favorite pasta or grain, and top with your favorite sauce. Enjoy!
Note: These lentil meatballs can also be frozen for later use. Simply place them on a baking sheet and freeze until solid, then transfer them to an airtight container or freezer bag. To reheat, simply bake them in a preheated oven at 400°F (200°C) for 10-15 minutes, or until heated through.

# Crispy Quinoa Cakes

Ingredients:

1 cup (180g) uncooked quinoa
2 cups (480 ml) water
1/2 cup (50 g) panko breadcrumbs (or other breadcrumbs of your choice)
1/2 cup (60 g) all-purpose flour
1/4 cup (30 g) nutritional yeast
1/4 cup (60 ml) olive oil
1/4 cup (60 ml) water
2 cloves of garlic, minced
1 small onion, chopped
1 tsp (5 ml) salt
1/2 tsp (2.5 ml) black pepper
1/4 tsp (1.25 ml) cayenne pepper (optional)
Vegetable oil for frying

Instructions:

Rinse the quinoa in a fine-mesh strainer and place it in a medium saucepan with 2 cups of water. Bring the water to a boil over high heat, then reduce the heat to low and simmer, covered, for 15-20 minutes or until the water has been absorbed and the quinoa is tender. Let the quinoa cool.

In a large mixing bowl, combine the cooled quinoa, panko breadcrumbs, all-purpose flour, nutritional yeast, garlic, onion, salt, black pepper, and cayenne pepper (if using). Mix everything together until well combined.
In a separate small bowl, whisk together the olive oil and 1/4 cup of water. Pour this mixture over the quinoa mixture and mix everything together until well combined.
Use your hands to form the quinoa mixture into 2-3 inch (5-7.5 cm) wide patties, about 1/2 inch (1.25 cm) thick.
Heat enough vegetable oil in a large frying pan over medium-high heat. Once the oil is hot, carefully place the quinoa cakes in the pan, making sure not to overcrowd them. Cook for 2-3 minutes on each side, or until golden brown and crispy.
Once cooked, place the quinoa cakes on a paper towel-lined plate to absorb any excess oil.
Serve the crispy quinoa cakes with a side salad or your favorite dipping sauce. Enjoy!
Note: These quinoa cakes can also be baked in the oven at 375°F (190°C) for 20-25 minutes, or until golden brown and crispy.

# Vegan Ramen

Ingredients:

4 cups (960 ml) of vegetable broth
2 cloves of garlic, minced
1-inch (2.5 cm) piece of ginger, peeled and grated
1 tbsp (15 ml) of soy sauce or tamari
1 tbsp (15 ml) of miso paste
1 tsp (5 ml) of sesame oil
1/2 tsp (2.5 ml) of chili flakes (optional)
1 block of ramen noodles (or other noodles of your choice)
1 small carrot, julienned
1/2 cup (50 g) of sliced shiitake mushrooms
1/2 cup (50 g) of sliced green onions
1/2 cup (50 g) of chopped bok choy
1/2 cup (120 g) of firm tofu, cubed
Salt and black pepper, to taste

Instructions:

In a large pot, bring the vegetable broth, garlic, ginger, soy sauce or tamari, miso paste, sesame oil, and chili flakes (if using) to a boil over high heat.
Reduce the heat to low and let the broth simmer for 15-20 minutes.
While the broth is simmering, cook the ramen noodles according to the package instructions. Drain and set aside.
Add the julienned carrot, sliced shiitake mushrooms, chopped bok choy, and cubed tofu to the simmering broth. Let everything cook for another 5-7 minutes, or until the vegetables are tender.
To assemble the ramen bowls, divide the cooked noodles between 4 bowls. Pour the vegetable broth and vegetables over the noodles. Top each bowl with sliced green onions and black pepper, to taste.
Serve the vegan ramen immediately and enjoy!
Note: You can add any other vegetables or toppings that you like to your vegan ramen, such as sliced bell peppers, bean sprouts, nori seaweed, or pickled ginger.

# Pesto Pasta

Ingredients:

1 pound (450 g) of pasta (such as spaghetti or linguine)
2 cups (80 g) of fresh basil leaves, packed
1/2 cup (75 g) of pine nuts or walnuts
3 cloves of garlic, peeled
1/2 cup (120 ml) of olive oil
1/2 cup (40 g) of nutritional yeast
1 tsp (5 ml) of lemon juice
Salt and black pepper, to taste

Instructions:

Cook the pasta according to the package instructions. Drain and set aside.
While the pasta is cooking, prepare the pesto sauce. In a food processor or blender, combine the basil leaves, pine nuts or walnuts, and garlic. Pulse until everything is chopped.
With the food processor or blender running, slowly drizzle in the olive oil until the mixture becomes a smooth paste.
Add the nutritional yeast and lemon juice to the pesto sauce and pulse until everything is well combined.
Season the pesto sauce with salt and black pepper, to taste.
Toss the cooked pasta with the pesto sauce until everything is well coated.
Serve the vegan pesto pasta hot, with extra nutritional yeast and chopped fresh basil on top, if desired. Enjoy!

# Vegan Pizza

Ingredients:

1 pizza crust (homemade or store-bought)
1/2 cup (120 ml) of tomato sauce
1/2 cup (75 g) of sliced mushrooms
1/2 cup (75 g) of sliced bell peppers
1/2 cup (50 g) of sliced red onions
1/2 cup (30 g) of chopped artichoke hearts
1/2 cup (80 g) of sliced black olives
1/2 cup (30 g) of fresh basil leaves, chopped
1/2 cup (120 g) of vegan cheese shreds (such as Daiya or Follow Your Heart)
Salt and black pepper, to taste
Optional: red pepper flakes, vegan pepperoni, or other toppings of your choice

Instructions:

Preheat the oven to 425°F (220°C).
Place the pizza crust on a baking sheet or pizza stone.
Spread the tomato sauce over the pizza crust, leaving a 1/2-inch (1.3 cm) border around the edges.
Add the sliced mushrooms, bell peppers, red onions, chopped artichoke hearts, black olives, and chopped basil to the pizza. Season everything with salt and black pepper, to taste.
Sprinkle the vegan cheese shreds over the top of the pizza.
Bake the pizza in the preheated oven for 10-15 minutes, or until the cheese is melted and bubbly and the crust is golden brown.
Remove the pizza from the oven and let it cool for a few minutes before slicing and serving.
Top the pizza with red pepper flakes, vegan pepperoni, or other toppings of your choice, if desired.
Enjoy your delicious and healthy vegan pizza!

# Vegan Banana Fritters

Ingredients:

3 ripe bananas, mashed
1/2 cup (60 g) of all-purpose flour
1/4 cup (30 g) of cornstarch
1/4 cup (50 g) of granulated sugar
1 tsp (5 g) of baking powder
1/4 tsp (1.5 g) of salt
1/4 tsp (0.5 g) of ground cinnamon
1/4 cup (60 ml) of plant-based milk
Vegetable oil, for frying
Powdered sugar, for dusting

Instructions:

In a mixing bowl, combine the mashed bananas, flour, cornstarch, sugar, baking powder, salt, and cinnamon. Mix well until the batter is smooth.
Gradually add the plant-based milk to the batter, stirring until it is well incorporated and smooth.
Heat the vegetable oil in a deep frying pan over medium-high heat. The oil should be hot enough that a small drop of batter sizzles and floats to the surface immediately.
Use a spoon to drop the batter into the hot oil, making small fritters that are about 2-3 inches (5-7.5 cm) in diameter. Fry the fritters in batches, being careful not to overcrowd the pan.
Fry the fritters for about 2-3 minutes on each side, or until they are golden brown and crispy.
Use a slotted spoon to transfer the fritters to a paper towel-lined plate to drain any excess oil.
Repeat the frying process with the remaining batter until all the fritters are cooked.
Dust the crispy banana fritters with powdered sugar before serving.
Enjoy your crispy and sweet vegan banana fritters as a snack or dessert!

# Fluffy And Delicious Pancakes

Ingredients:

1 cup (120 g) of all-purpose flour
2 tbsp (25 g) of granulated sugar
2 tsp (10 g) of baking powder
1/2 tsp (2.5 g) of salt
1 cup (240 ml) of plant-based milk (such as almond or soy milk)
1 tbsp (15 ml) of apple cider vinegar
2 tbsp (30 ml) of vegetable oil
1 tsp (5 ml) of vanilla extract

Instructions:

In a mixing bowl, whisk together the flour, sugar, baking powder, and salt until well combined.
In a separate bowl, combine the plant-based milk and apple cider vinegar. Stir well and let sit for 2-3 minutes to curdle.
Add the vegetable oil and vanilla extract to the plant-based milk mixture and stir to combine.
Pour the wet ingredients into the dry ingredients and stir until just combined. Be careful not to overmix the batter, as this can make the pancakes tough.
Heat a non-stick pan or griddle over medium heat. Once hot, use a ladle or measuring cup to pour the pancake batter onto the pan. Cook for 2-3 minutes on each side, or until the pancakes are golden brown and cooked through.
Serve the vegan pancakes warm with your favorite toppings, such as fresh fruit, vegan butter, maple syrup, or vegan whipped cream.
Enjoy your delicious and fluffy vegan pancakes for breakfast or brunch!

# Vegan Scrambled Eggs

Ingredients:

1 block (14 oz/400 g) of firm tofu, drained and crumbled
2 tbsp (30 ml) of olive oil
1/2 onion, diced
2 cloves of garlic, minced
1/2 red bell pepper, diced
1/2 yellow bell pepper, diced
1 tsp (5 g) of turmeric
1 tsp (5 ml) of soy sauce
Salt and pepper, to taste
Fresh parsley, chopped (optional)

Instructions:

Heat the olive oil in a non-stick skillet over medium heat. Add the onion and garlic, and sauté for 2-3 minutes until softened.
Add the diced bell peppers to the skillet and cook for an additional 2-3 minutes until they are tender.
Add the crumbled tofu to the skillet and sprinkle with turmeric. Stir well to combine, and continue to cook for 5-7 minutes, stirring occasionally, until the tofu is lightly browned and crispy.
Add the soy sauce to the skillet and stir to combine. Season with salt and pepper to taste.
Continue to cook the tofu scramble for an additional 1-2 minutes until heated through.
Serve the vegan scrambled eggs hot, garnished with chopped parsley if desired.
Enjoy your delicious and healthy vegan scrambled eggs for breakfast or brunch!

# Delicious Vegan Lasagna

### Ingredients:

- 1 lb (454 g) of lasagna noodles
- 2 tbsp (30 ml) of olive oil
- 1 onion, diced
- 4 cloves of garlic, minced
- 1 bell pepper, diced
- 1 zucchini, diced
- 1 cup (150 g) of sliced mushrooms
- 2 cans (28 oz/794 g) of crushed tomatoes
- 2 tsp (10 g) of dried basil
- 1 tsp (5 g) of dried oregano
- 1/2 tsp (2.5 g) of salt
- 1/4 tsp (1.25 g) of black pepper
- 1 lb (454 g) of firm tofu, drained and crumbled
- 1/2 cup (50 g) of nutritional yeast
- 1 tsp (5 g) of garlic powder
- 2 tbsp (30 ml) of lemon juice
- 1/4 cup (60 ml) of plant-based milk (such as almond or soy milk)
- 2 cups (240 g) of vegan shredded cheese

### Instructions:

Preheat your oven to 375°F (190°C). Cook the lasagna noodles according to the package instructions until al dente. Drain and set aside.

In a large skillet, heat the olive oil over medium heat. Add the onion and garlic, and sauté for 2-3 minutes until softened.

Add the bell pepper, zucchini, and mushrooms to the skillet, and cook for an additional 5-7 minutes until they are tender.

Add the crushed tomatoes, basil, oregano, salt, and black pepper to the skillet. Stir well to combine and simmer for 10-15 minutes, stirring occasionally, until the sauce has thickened.

In a mixing bowl, combine the crumbled tofu, nutritional yeast, garlic powder, lemon juice, and plant-based milk. Stir well to combine.

Spread a layer of the tomato sauce in the bottom of a 9x13 inch baking dish. Layer with a single layer of cooked lasagna noodles, followed by a layer of the tofu mixture and a layer of shredded vegan cheese. Repeat the layers until all the ingredients are used up, ending with a layer of tomato sauce on top.

Cover the baking dish with foil and bake in the preheated oven for 30 minutes. Remove the foil and bake for an additional 10-15 minutes until the cheese is melted and bubbly.

Let the vegan lasagna cool for 5-10 minutes before serving.

Enjoy your delicious and hearty vegan lasagna!

# Vegan Quesadilla

Ingredients:

4 medium flour tortillas
1 can (15 oz/425 g) of black beans, drained and rinsed
1 red bell pepper, diced
1/2 red onion, diced
1 avocado, diced
1 jalapeño pepper, diced (optional)
1 tbsp (15 ml) of olive oil
1 tsp (5 g) of ground cumin
1/2 tsp (2.5 g) of garlic powder
Salt and pepper, to taste
Vegan shredded cheese (such as cheddar or mozzarella)

Instructions:

In a mixing bowl, combine the black beans, red bell pepper, red onion, avocado, jalapeño pepper (if using), olive oil, cumin, garlic powder, salt, and pepper. Stir well to combine.
Heat a large skillet over medium heat. Place one tortilla in the skillet and sprinkle with a thin layer of vegan shredded cheese. Spoon a quarter of the black bean mixture onto one half of the tortilla.
Fold the tortilla over the filling to create a half-moon shape. Press down lightly with a spatula to seal the edges.
Cook the vegan quesadilla for 2-3 minutes on each side until golden brown and crispy. Repeat with the remaining tortillas and black bean mixture.
Cut the vegan quesadillas into wedges and serve hot.
Enjoy your delicious and healthy vegan quesadillas for lunch or dinner! You can also serve them with salsa, guacamole, or vegan sour cream for added flavor.

# Vegan Scones

Ingredients:

2 cups (240 g) of all-purpose flour
1/3 cup (67 g) of granulated sugar
1 tbsp (15 ml) of baking powder
1/2 tsp (2.5 g) of baking soda
1/2 tsp (2.5 g) of salt
1/2 cup (113 g) of vegan butter, chilled and cubed
1/2 cup (120 ml) of unsweetened plant-based milk (such as almond or soy milk)
1 tbsp (15 ml) of apple cider vinegar
1 tsp (5 ml) of vanilla extract
1/2 cup (75 g) of dried fruit or nuts (such as raisins, cranberries, or chopped almonds) (optional)
Vegan cream or jam, for serving (optional)

Instructions:

Preheat your oven to 400°F (200°C) and line a baking sheet with parchment paper.
In a mixing bowl, whisk together the flour, sugar, baking powder, baking soda, and salt.
Using a pastry cutter or your fingers, cut the vegan butter into the flour mixture until it resembles coarse crumbs.
In a separate mixing bowl, whisk together the plant-based milk, apple cider vinegar, and vanilla extract.
Pour the wet ingredients into the dry ingredients and stir until just combined. Do not overmix.
If using, fold in the dried fruit or nuts.
Transfer the scone dough to a lightly floured surface and knead it gently a few times until it comes together. Do not overwork the dough.
Using your hands or a rolling pin, flatten the dough into a circle about 1 inch (2.5 cm) thick.
Using a sharp knife or a biscuit cutter, cut the dough into 8-10 wedges.
Place the scones on the prepared baking sheet and bake for 15-18 minutes, or until golden brown and cooked through.
Let the vegan scones cool on the baking sheet for a few minutes before transferring them to a wire rack to cool completely.
Serve the scones warm or at room temperature with vegan cream or jam, if desired.
Enjoy your delicious and easy-to-make vegan scones for breakfast, brunch, or a snack!

# Vegan Burritos

Ingredients:

1 cup (185 g) of uncooked brown rice
1 can (15 oz/425 g) of black beans, drained and rinsed
1 red bell pepper, diced
1/2 red onion, diced
1 avocado, diced
1 jalapeño pepper, diced (optional)
1 tbsp (15 ml) of olive oil
1 tsp (5 g) of ground cumin
1/2 tsp (2.5 g) of garlic powder
Salt and pepper, to taste
4-6 large flour tortillas
Vegan shredded cheese (such as cheddar or mozzarella) (optional)
Salsa, guacamole, or vegan sour cream, for serving (optional)

Instructions:

Cook the brown rice according to the package instructions.
In a mixing bowl, combine the black beans, red bell pepper, red onion, avocado, jalapeño pepper (if using), olive oil, cumin, garlic powder, salt, and pepper. Stir well to combine.
Heat a large skillet over medium heat. Add the black bean mixture to the skillet and cook for 5-7 minutes, stirring occasionally, until the vegetables are tender and the beans are heated through.
Warm the flour tortillas in the microwave or oven.
To assemble the vegan burritos, place a spoonful of brown rice in the center of each tortilla, followed by a spoonful of the black bean mixture. If using, sprinkle vegan shredded cheese on top.
Fold the sides of the tortilla over the filling, then roll it up tightly.
Repeat with the remaining tortillas and filling.
Serve the vegan burritos with salsa, guacamole, or vegan sour cream, if desired.
Enjoy your delicious and filling vegan burritos for lunch or dinner! You can also customize them by adding your favorite vegetables or toppings.

# Vegan Sausage Rolls

Ingredients:

For the filling:

1 can (15 oz/425 g) of chickpeas, drained and rinsed
1/2 cup (50 g) of rolled oats
1/4 cup (30 g) of nutritional yeast
1 tbsp (15 ml) of soy sauce
1 tsp (5 g) of smoked paprika
1 tsp (5 g) of garlic powder
1/2 tsp (2.5 g) of dried thyme
1/4 tsp (1.25 g) of cayenne pepper (optional)
Salt and pepper, to taste

For the pastry:

1 sheet of vegan puff pastry, thawed
1 tbsp (15 ml) of non-dairy milk

Instructions:

Preheat the oven to 375°F (190°C).

In a food processor, pulse the chickpeas, rolled oats, nutritional yeast, soy sauce, smoked paprika, garlic powder, thyme, cayenne pepper (if using), salt, and pepper until the mixture is smooth and forms a paste.
Roll out the puff pastry on a lightly floured surface into a large rectangle.
Cut the pastry in half lengthwise to create two long rectangles.
Divide the filling mixture in half, and roll each half into a log shape, placing it lengthwise on each rectangle of pastry.
Brush the edges of the pastry with non-dairy milk.
Roll the pastry up tightly around the filling, pressing the edges together to seal.
Cut the pastry rolls into smaller pieces, about 1-2 inches (2.5-5 cm) each.
Place the pastry rolls on a baking sheet lined with parchment paper.
Brush the tops of the pastry rolls with non-dairy milk.
Bake the vegan sausage rolls in the oven for 25-30 minutes, or until they are golden brown and crispy.
Serve hot, and enjoy your delicious vegan sausage rolls as a snack or appetizer!
These vegan sausage rolls are a great alternative to traditional sausage rolls, and they are easy to make and perfect for sharing. You can also customize the filling with your favorite spices and herbs.

# Paprika Roasted Potato Wedges

Here's a recipe for paprika roasted potato wedges that are crispy, flavorful and perfect as a side dish or snack:

Ingredients:

4 medium-sized potatoes, washed and cut into wedges
1 tbsp (15 ml) olive oil
1 tsp (5 g) garlic powder
1 tsp (5 g) smoked paprika
1/2 tsp (2.5 g) salt
Freshly ground black pepper, to taste

Instructions:
Preheat the oven to 400°F (200°C).
In a mixing bowl, whisk together the olive oil, garlic powder, smoked paprika, salt, and black pepper.
Add the potato wedges to the bowl and toss them with the spice mixture until they are evenly coated.
Place the potato wedges in a single layer on a baking sheet lined with parchment paper.
Bake the potato wedges in the oven for 25-30 minutes, or until they are golden brown and crispy.
Remove the potato wedges from the oven and let them cool for a few minutes before serving.
Serve your delicious paprika roasted potato wedges as a side dish or snack, garnished with fresh herbs if desired.
These paprika roasted potato wedges are easy to make, healthy and packed with flavor. You can adjust the amount of spices to your liking or add your favorite herbs for extra flavor. Enjoy!

# Ginger Loaf Cake

Ingredients:

2 cups all-purpose flour
1 tsp baking powder
1 tsp baking soda
1/2 tsp salt
1 tbsp ground ginger
1 tsp ground cinnamon
1/4 tsp ground nutmeg
1/2 cup vegetable oil
1/2 cup molasses
1/2 cup brown sugar
1 cup unsweetened almond milk
1 tbsp apple cider vinegar

Instructions:

Preheat your oven to 350°F (175°C) and grease a 9x5 inch loaf pan.
In a large bowl, whisk together the flour, baking powder, baking soda, salt, ginger, cinnamon, and nutmeg until well combined.
In another bowl, whisk together the vegetable oil, molasses, brown sugar, almond milk, and apple cider vinegar until well combined.
Pour the wet ingredients into the dry ingredients and stir until just combined. Do not overmix.
Pour the batter into the prepared loaf pan and bake for 45-50 minutes, or until a toothpick inserted into the center of the cake comes out clean.
Let the cake cool in the pan for 10 minutes before transferring it to a wire rack to cool completely.
Serve the ginger loaf cake sliced and enjoy!
Optional: If you want to add some extra sweetness, you can make a simple glaze by whisking together 1 cup powdered sugar and 2-3 tbsp almond milk until smooth. Drizzle the glaze over the cooled cake before serving.
ChatGPT Feb 13 Version. Free Research Preview. Our goal is to make AI systems more natural and safe to interact with. Your feedback will help us improve.

# Apple Cake

Ingredients:

2 cups all-purpose flour
1 1/2 cups granulated sugar
2 tsp baking powder
1 tsp baking soda
1 tsp ground cinnamon
1/2 tsp ground nutmeg
1/2 tsp salt
1/2 cup vegetable oil
1/2 cup unsweetened applesauce
1/4 cup non-dairy milk (such as almond or soy milk)
1 tsp vanilla extract
2 cups peeled and diced apples
1 tbsp lemon juice
Powdered sugar (for dusting)

Instructions:

Preheat your oven to 350°F (175°C). Grease a 9-inch (23 cm) cake pan with vegetable oil.
In a large mixing bowl, whisk together the flour, sugar, baking powder, baking soda, cinnamon, nutmeg, and salt.
In a separate mixing bowl, combine the vegetable oil, applesauce, non-dairy milk, and vanilla extract. Mix well.
Add the wet mixture to the dry mixture and stir until just combined. Don't overmix.
In a small bowl, mix together the diced apples and lemon juice. Fold the apple mixture into the batter.
Pour the batter into the prepared cake pan and smooth out the top.
Bake the cake for 50-60 minutes or until a toothpick inserted into the center comes out clean.
Let the cake cool in the pan for 10 minutes, then transfer it to a wire rack to cool completely.
Dust the top of the cake with powdered sugar.
Slice and serve!
Enjoy your delicious vegan apple cake!

# Bean Chilli Fries

Ingredients:

For the Chili:

1 tbsp olive oil
1 onion, diced
2 garlic cloves, minced
1 bell pepper, diced
1 jalapeno pepper, seeded and minced (optional)
1 can of diced tomatoes (14 oz)
1 can of black beans, drained and rinsed (14 oz)
1 can of kidney beans, drained and rinsed (14 oz)
2 tsp chili powder
1 tsp ground cumin
1/2 tsp smoked paprika
1/2 tsp salt
1/4 tsp black pepper
1/4 cup water
1 tbsp tomato paste
1 tbsp lime juice

For the Fries:

4-6 large potatoes, cut into fries
1 tbsp olive oil
1 tsp chili powder
1/2 tsp smoked paprika
1/2 tsp garlic powder
Salt and pepper, to taste

Instructions:

Preheat the oven to 425°F (220°C).
In a large skillet, heat 1 tablespoon of olive oil over medium-high heat. Add the onion, garlic, bell pepper, and jalapeno pepper (if using). Cook for 5-7 minutes, until the vegetables are tender.
Add the diced tomatoes, black beans, kidney beans, chili powder, cumin, smoked paprika, salt, and black pepper. Stir to combine.
Add 1/4 cup of water and tomato paste, and stir until combined. Let the mixture simmer for 10-15 minutes, stirring occasionally, until the chili has thickened.
Add the lime juice and stir to combine. Taste and adjust seasonings as needed.
Meanwhile, in a large mixing bowl, combine the potatoes, olive oil, chili powder, smoked paprika, garlic powder, salt, and pepper. Toss until the fries are evenly coated.
Spread the fries out in a single layer on a baking sheet lined with parchment paper.
Bake the fries for 20-25 minutes, until they are crispy and golden brown.
Remove the fries from the oven and top with the chili.
Serve immediately and enjoy your delicious vegan bean chili fries!

# Vegan Brownies

Ingredients:

1 cup all-purpose flour
1 cup granulated sugar
1/2 cup unsweetened cocoa powder
1 teaspoon baking powder
1/2 teaspoon salt
1/2 cup vegetable oil
1/2 cup unsweetened applesauce
1 teaspoon vanilla extract
1/2 cup vegan chocolate chips

Instructions:

Preheat the oven to 350°F (180°C) and line an 8x8 inch baking pan with parchment paper.
In a large mixing bowl, whisk together the flour, sugar, cocoa powder, baking powder, and salt.
Add the vegetable oil, applesauce, and vanilla extract to the dry ingredients and stir until well combined.
Fold in the vegan chocolate chips.
Pour the batter into the prepared baking pan and smooth the surface with a spatula.
Bake for 25-30 minutes, or until a toothpick inserted in the center comes out clean.
Let the brownies cool in the pan for 10 minutes, then transfer them to a wire rack to cool completely.
Once cooled, slice the brownies into desired serving size and enjoy!
These vegan brownies are rich, chocolatey, and indulgent. They're perfect for satisfying your sweet tooth without any animal products. Enjoy!

# Banana Bread

Ingredients:

3 ripe bananas, mashed
1/4 cup vegan butter, melted
1/4 cup unsweetened applesauce
1/2 cup granulated sugar
1 teaspoon vanilla extract
1 1/2 cups all-purpose flour
1 teaspoon baking soda
1/2 teaspoon salt
1/2 teaspoon ground cinnamon
Optional add-ins: chopped nuts, chocolate chips, or dried fruit

Directions:

Preheat your oven to 350°F (175°C). Grease a 9x5 inch loaf pan or line it with parchment paper.
In a mixing bowl, combine the mashed bananas, melted vegan butter, applesauce, granulated sugar, and vanilla extract. Stir until well-combined.
In a separate mixing bowl, whisk together the flour, baking soda, salt, and ground cinnamon.
Gradually stir the dry ingredients into the wet mixture until just combined. If you're adding any optional add-ins, fold them in now.
Pour the batter into the prepared loaf pan.
Bake for 50-60 minutes or until a toothpick inserted into the center of the bread comes out clean.
Let the bread cool in the pan for 10-15 minutes before removing it from the pan and placing it on a wire rack to cool completely.
Slice and serve the vegan banana bread as desired. Enjoy!
Note: This recipe is easily customizable! Feel free to add in your favorite nuts, chocolate chips, or dried fruit to give it an extra burst of flavor.

# Margherita Pizza

Ingredients:

1 batch of pizza dough (store-bought or homemade)
1/2 cup tomato sauce
1/2 teaspoon dried oregano
1/4 teaspoon garlic powder
1/4 teaspoon salt
1/4 teaspoon black pepper
1/2 cup vegan mozzarella cheese, shredded
1 large tomato, thinly sliced
Fresh basil leaves, chopped

Instructions:

Preheat your oven to 425°F (220°C). If you have a pizza stone, place it in the oven while it preheats.
Roll out your pizza dough on a floured surface until it's about 1/4 inch thick. Transfer the dough to a piece of parchment paper.
In a small bowl, mix together the tomato sauce, oregano, garlic powder, salt, and black pepper. Spread the mixture over the pizza dough, leaving a small border around the edges.
Sprinkle the shredded vegan mozzarella cheese over the sauce.
Arrange the tomato slices on top of the cheese.
Transfer the pizza on the parchment paper to the preheated pizza stone or a baking sheet.
Bake the pizza for 10-12 minutes, or until the crust is golden brown and the cheese is melted and bubbly.
Remove the pizza from the oven and sprinkle with fresh chopped basil.
Slice and serve hot.
Enjoy your delicious and vegan-friendly margherita pizza!

# Vegan Fajitas

Ingredients:

1 red bell pepper, sliced
1 green bell pepper, sliced
1 yellow onion, sliced
1 tbsp olive oil
1 tsp ground cumin
1 tsp chili powder
1/2 tsp paprika
1/4 tsp garlic powder
1/4 tsp onion powder
Salt and pepper, to taste
4-6 tortillas (flour or corn)
Optional toppings: diced avocado, fresh cilantro, salsa, hot sauce, vegan sour cream

Instructions:

Heat a large skillet over medium heat. Add olive oil, bell peppers, and onion. Sauté for 5-7 minutes, or until the vegetables are tender.
In a small bowl, mix together the ground cumin, chili powder, paprika, garlic powder, onion powder, salt, and pepper.
Sprinkle the spice mixture over the vegetables, stirring well to coat. Cook for an additional 2-3 minutes, or until the spices are fragrant and the vegetables are evenly coated.
Warm up the tortillas in the oven, microwave, or on a dry skillet.
Assemble the fajitas by spooning the vegetable mixture onto the center of each tortilla. Add optional toppings such as diced avocado, fresh cilantro, salsa, hot sauce, and/or vegan sour cream, if desired.
Serve hot and enjoy your delicious vegan fajitas!

I want to take a moment to express my heartfelt gratitude for your recent purchase of my recipe book. As a passionate food lover, nothing makes me happier than sharing my favorite recipes with others. Your decision to invest in my book not only supports my dream, but also shows your commitment to expanding your culinary horizons.

I sincerely hope that the recipes in the book will inspire you to try new things and add some excitement to your meals.

Thank you again for your support and for being a part of this journey with me. I hope my book will bring you many happy and delicious moments in the kitchen.

www.ingramcontent.com/pod-product-compliance
Lightning Source LLC
Chambersburg PA
CBHW041151110526
44590CB00027B/4198